First Day at School

Monica Hughes

 Raintree

Chicago, Illinois

© 2004 Raintree
Published by Raintree, a division of Reed Elsevier, Inc.
Chicago, Illinois
Customer Service 888-363-4266
Visit our website at www.raintreelibrary.com

Printed and bound in the United States at Lake Book Manufacturing, Inc.
07 06 05 04
10 9 8 7 6 5 4 3 2

Library of Congress Cataloging-in-Publication Data:
Hughes, Monica.
  First day at school / Monica Hughes.
     p. cm. -- (My first)
Includes bibliographical references and index.
Contents: Before school -- In the coatroom -- In the classroom -- Everyone is busy -- Playtime -- Back to the classroom -- Lunchtime -- Afternoon activities -- The day ends -- Home time.
  ISBN 1-4109-0643-4 (lib. bdg.) -- ISBN 1-4109-0669-8 (pbk.)
  1. First day of school--Juvenile literature. 2. Early childhood education--Juvenile literature. [1. First day of school. 2. Schools.]
I. Title. II. Series: Hughes, Monica. My first.
  LB1139.23.H84 2004
  371'.002--dc21
                              2003011052

Acknowledgments
The Publishers would like to thank Gareth Boden for permission to reproduce all the photographs that appear in this book.

The cover photograph is reproduced with permission of Gareth Boden

Some words are shown in bold, **like this.** You can find out what they mean by looking in the glossary on page 24.

Contents

Before School

This is Anna.
She is getting ready for
her first day of school.

4

This is Andy.
This is his first
day, too.

Good Morning!

Anna hangs up her coat.
She meets a new teacher.

Andy goes to his classroom.
He tells his mom and sister goodbye.

7

In the Classroom

Anna reads her name.
This is her **drawer**.

Andy listens to the teacher.

9

Reading and Writing

Anna and her class read a poem.

Andy learns to write some letters.

Math and Art

Anna and her class learn
about the number four.

Andy and his class make clay art.

13

Recess

We put on our coats to go outside for recess.

Andy plays on the playground.

Time for Lunch

Anna brings her lunch to school.

She has a new **lunchbox**.

Andy buys his lunch at school.

Afternoon

Anna and her friends play at the **water table.**

Andy pastes.

His friends paint.

Library and Music

Anna's class goes to the **library**.
Anna reads a book.

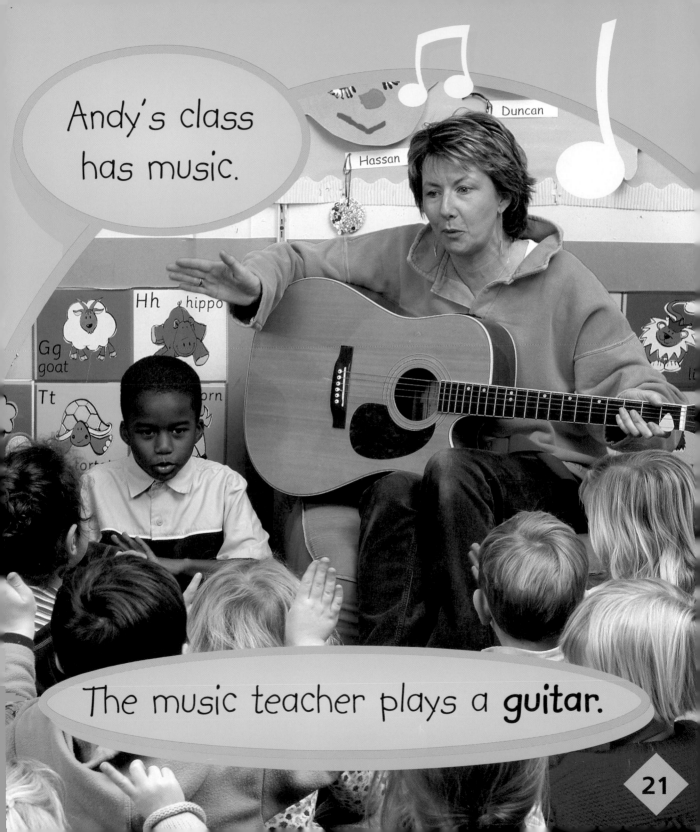

Time to Go Home

Anna says goodbye to her new friends.

She takes her **lunchbox** home.

Grace   Alex

Andy is asleep.

What a busy day at school!

Glossary

drawer (You say DROH-r.)
a special place to keep your things

guitar (You say gih-TAHR.)
a musical instrument made of wood played by strumming on the strings

library a place where you can borrow books and magazines

lunchbox a container you can use to bring your lunch to school

water table a big box that can be filled with water

Index